LET'S BE BOLDLY BEARCAT

by
Kimberlee Dobbs

University of
CINCINNATI | CLIPS

About the University of Cincinnati Library Publishing Services

CLIPS provides professional publishing services for conference proceedings, journals, affordable textbooks and open educational resources produced by UC faculty, staff, and UC organizations with department sponsorship and funding. CLIPS is an imprint of the University of Cincinnati Press, which is committed to publishing rigorous, peer–reviewed, leading scholarship in social justice, community engagement, and Cincinnati/Ohio history.

The University of Cincinnati Press and Library Publishing Services
Copyright © 2019

Published in 2019

ISBN 978-1-947603-05-9 (paperback)

Library of Congress Control Number: 2019939216

Designed and typeset for UC Press by Alisa Strauss
Typeset in: Rift and Poppins
Printed in the United States of America
First Printing

I am boldly Bearcat.
Let's be boldly Bearcat together!

COLLEGE OF
EDUCATION, CRIMINAL JUSTICE, AND HUMAN SERVICES

A boldly Bearcat likes to learn. What do you like to learn?

A boldly Bearcat likes to have fun and exercise. What do you do to have fun?

A boldly Bearcat likes to eat healthy food. What healthy foods do you like to eat?

A boldly Bearcat likes to create new things. What do you like to create?

A boldly Bearcat likes to help people when they are sick. What do you do to help someone who is not feeling well?

A boldly Bearcat likes to explore. What do you like to explore?

A boldly Bearcat likes to sing and dance. Do you like music? What is your favorite song?

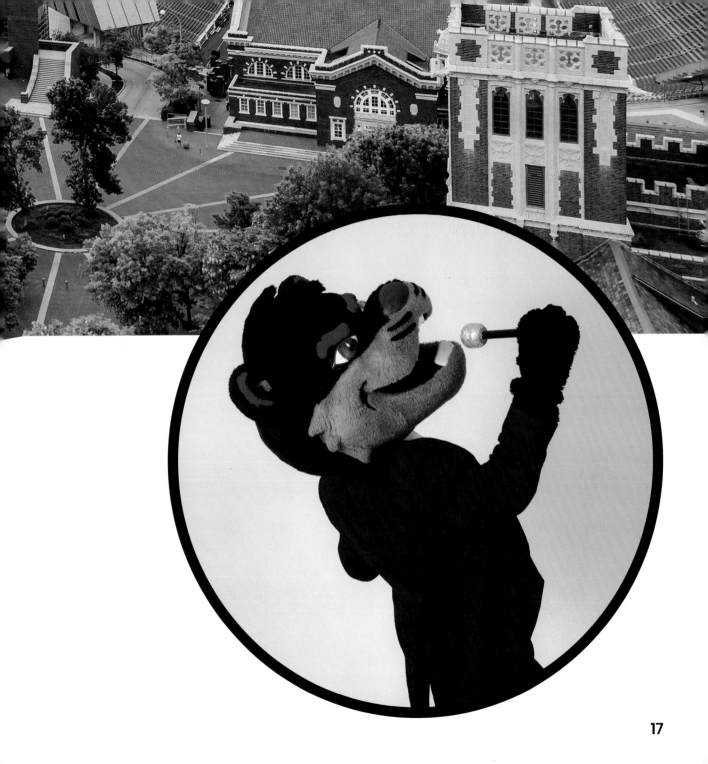

A boldly Bearcat likes to build things. What do you like to build?

CARL H. LINDNER COLLEGE OF BUSINESS

A boldly Bearcat likes numbers. Do you like to count? Let's count!

A boldly Bearcat likes to follow rules to keep safe. What rules do you need to follow?

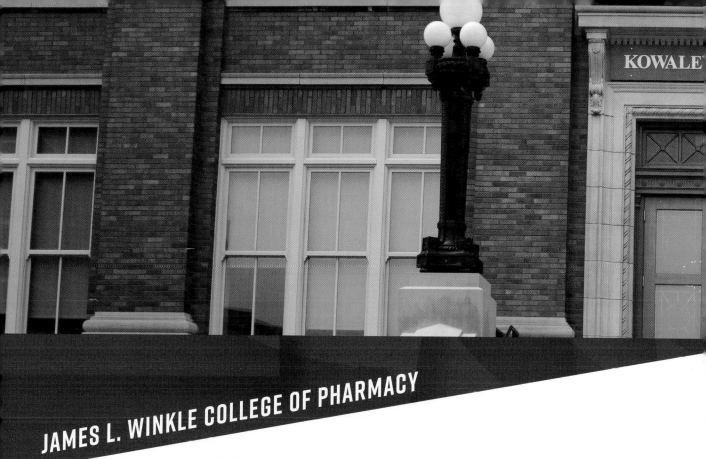

JAMES L. WINKLE COLLEGE OF PHARMACY

KOWALE

A boldly Bearcat likes to help others feel better. How can you make others feel better?

24

COLLEGE OF MEDICINE

A boldly Bearcat likes to care for others. How do you care for others?

A boldly Bearcat likes to have a nice smile. What do you do to take care of your teeth?

UC CLERMONT COLLEGE

A boldly Bearcat likes to be helpful in the community. Who are some community helpers where you live?

I want to learn _____

_____

_____.

DRAW IT!

I have fun when _____

_____

_____ .

DRAW IT!

I like to eat _____

_____

_____.

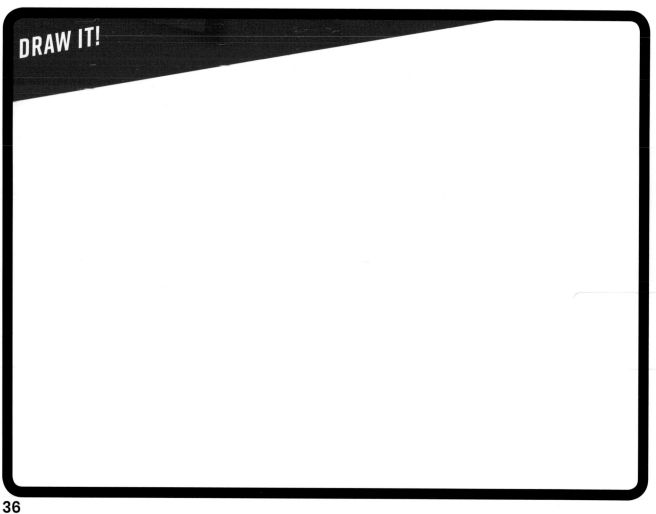

DRAW IT!

I like to create _____

_____

_____.

DRAW IT!

I am kind when _____

_____

_____.

DRAW IT!

I like to explore _____

_____

_____ .

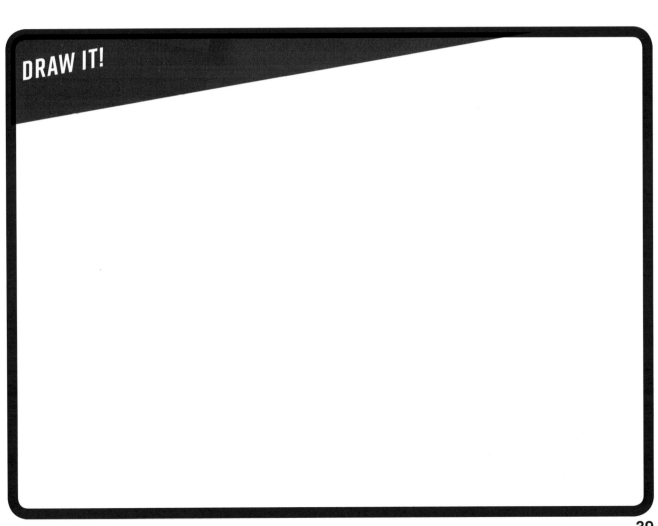

DRAW IT!

My favorite song is _____

_____

_____.

DRAW IT!

I can build _____

_____

_____.

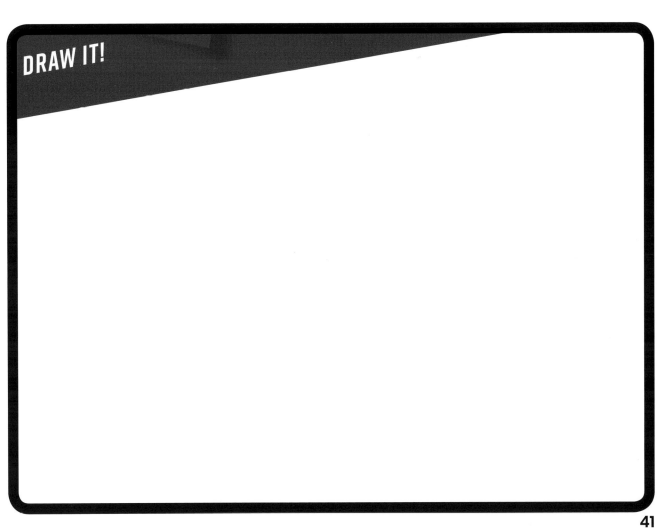

DRAW IT!

I can count to _____

_____

_____.

DRAW IT!

An important rule to follow is

_____

_____ .

DRAW IT!

I can make others feel better by _____

_____.

DRAW IT!

I can show I care by _____

_____

_____.

DRAW IT!

I take care of my teeth by _____

_____

_____.

DRAW IT!

I can be helpful by _____

_____

_____ .

DRAW IT!

CAN YOU FIND IT?

A boldly Bearcat likes to find places on a map. Can you find these places?

1 College of Design, Architecture, Art, and Planning
2 Geology-Physics Building
3 Braunstein Hall
4 McMicken Hall
5 College of Education, Criminal Justice, and Human Resources
6 College of Law
7 Blegen Library
8 College-Conservatory of Music
9 Tangeman University Center
10 Baldwin Hall
11 Zimmer Hall
12 Langsam Library
13 College of Engineering and Applied Science
14 Campus Rec Center
15 Nippert Stadium
16 Fifth Third Arena
17 Lindner College of Business
18 Marian Spencer Hall

BearCatch stop Download the BearCatch app to your phone or mobile device to explore unique and historic places around campus.

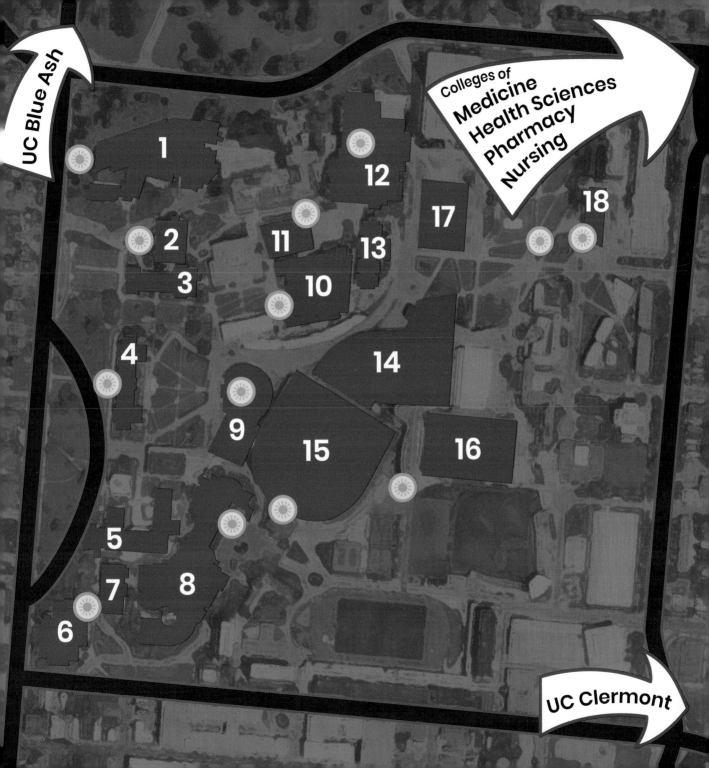

UC Blue Ash

Colleges of
**Medicine
Health Sciences
Pharmacy
Nursing**

UC Clermont

Dedicated to my family, Justin, Brandon, Lyndsee, Kyle, Katie, Greyson, Kynslee, Reagan, and Gavin.

In memory of Robert Dobbs.

All author royalties are being donated to University of Cincinnati scholarships.

ACKNOWLEDGEMENTS

Many thanks go to the following Bearcats:

- **Elizabeth Scarpelli** and UC Press for walking me through the process with knowledge, patience, and humor
- **Alisa Strauss** for setting up the pages with enthusiasm
- **Sarah Muncy** for her support in getting this project completed
- **Jace Bovenzi**, along with **Chad Archdeacon**, **Grant Rebadow**, and **Mikele Boyd** for being "Bearcatty"
- **Ravenna Rutledge**, a photographer with a bright future
- **DQuez Carr** and **Isaac Miller** for getting the word out about the book
- **Lisa Ventre** for her guidance and recommending star intern, Ravenna
- President's office and **Nicholas Scarpelli** for the building photographs
- **Stacie Kearns** for her painting of McMicken Hall (prints available at StacieKearnsart.com)
- **Greyson Ballinger**, **Kynslee Ballinger**, and **Eris Gibbons** for being cooperative during the photo shoot and for just being so cute

Author Kimberlee Dobbs with the staff of University of Cincinnati Press and Cincinnati Library Publishing Services (CLIPS).

Back row, left to right: DQuez Carr (UC Press sales intern and UC business student), Dr. Alisa Strauss (UC Press designer and instructor in Anthropology), Kimberlee Dobbs (author and CECH graduate '78). Elizabeth Scarpelli (UC Press director and CECH master's student), Sarah Muncy (UC Press assistant managing editor and A&S master's graduate '18), Ravenna Rutledge (photographer and UC DAAP '19)

Front row: Bearcat

Image Credits:

Pete Bender: UC Blue Ash College
Lisa Britton: College of Engineering and Applied Science
Joseph Fuqua II: College of Education Criminal Justice, and Human Services
Andrew Higley: Nippert Stadium
Ravenna Rutledge: all photos of the Bearcat, children, and adults

Nicholas Scarpelli: Colleges of Allied Health Sciences, Design, Architecture, Art, and Planning, Nursing, Arts and Sciences, Business, Pharmacy, UC Clermont
Alisa Strauss: UC campus map, cover photo, College of Law
Jay Yocis: Fifth Third Arena, College-Conservatory of Music, College of Medicine

ABOUT THE AUTHOR

Kimberlee Dobbs holds a bachelor's degree in Elementary Education from the University of Cincinnati. She holds a Master's degree in Reading. During her tenure as a teacher, she helped write the *Sounds Great!* phonics program which has helped thousands of students learn to read and write. This is Kimberlee's third publication, including *Looking for Bobby Bearcat*, published in 1996.

Kimberlee met her husband Robert on a blind date when he asked her to the Homecoming Dance at the University of Cincinnati. This started their lifelong commitment to give back to the university. Today, Kimberlee loves spending time with son Justin and daughter-in-law Katie, son Brandon, and daughter Lyndsee and son-in-law Kyle. Her pride and joy are her four grandchildren, Greyson, Kynslee, Reagan, and Gavin.

Kimberlee continues to be an extremely active member of the Bearcat community. She led the celebration committee for the reopening of Nippert Stadium and is current co-chair of UC's Bicentennial Committee. She is a member of the UC Foundation Board.